Walks of Life

WALKS OF LIFE
POEMS BY JANET ADELAIDE MACMAHON HICKMAN

Edited by E. Stewart Hickman

Ptarmigan House

Ptarmigan House
Silver Spring, Maryland USA
www.StewartHickman.com

Cover design by Victoria Heath Silk (VictoriaHeathSilk.com)
Cover art: La Porte Ouverte II, copper-plate etching and aquatint © Lynn Shaler, 1985
Book design and typesetting by Studio26 (insidestudio26.com)

Walks of Life: poems by Janet Adelaide MacMahon Hickman. -- 1st ed.
ISBN 979-8-9857393-2-9

Thanks

*To my sisters, Martha and Pat, for their help and
encouragement in pulling this volume together.*

*To Lynn Shaler, artist/engraver. Several of her works were part of
Janet's substantial and eclectic art collection. With permission from
the artist, her work, "La Porte Ouverte II," appears on the cover.*

*To Victoria Heath Silk for cover design and typesetting, who with
heart and skill crafted a volume better than what I had in mind.*

Contents

Preface

Born in Niagara Falls, N.Y. in 1922, Janet Adelaide MacMahon Hickman received a B.A. in English and Journalism from Syracuse University in 1944 and moved to Wilmington, Delaware later that year. She died in Hockessin, Delaware in 2006.

Janet's uniqueness lay partly in her gifts as an inquisitive, engaging and empathetic listener. Professionally she applied these in a variety of settings, including Director of Religious Education for the First Unitarian Church, and volunteer social worker and pastoral care counselor at area hospitals. Even in private life her encounters with people from all walks of life elicited their stories, which she invited by a demeanor of hospitable openness.

Janet's life and home were filled with the manifestations of her artistic interests and talents. She was a music lover and an accomplished pianist, and a member of area church choirs. Her alto voice enlivened many gatherings. A discerning collector of local modern art works and fine crafts with a flair for their display, Janet had a painter's eye for every scene she encountered. She was a voracious and eclectic reader. Her poetic work offers glimpses of life with a precise brevity that reflects her playfulness and her passion for language, art, landscape and people.

The first section of this volume represents poems from manila folders labeled *Poetry – work sheets*, and *Work folder*. An accurate chronology being a challenge (most poems are undated), I have arranged this first section from earliest adult writing to later work, roughly 1962 to 1987, as best as I could determine.

The source of the second and third sections is "*The Reluctant Lady* and other poems," which was assembled in a limited edition in honor of her eightieth birthday, in 2002. The source of *that* collection was Janet's poetry binder in which she had stored typed drafts of 24 poems that appear to have been revisited and revised over the years, and ten haiku.

The second section contains the haiku and senryu from "*The Reluctant Lady* and other poems." Both forms are based on Japanese traditional 3-line poetry – haiku is typically about the natural world; senryu, about human nature.

The third section contains the remainder of the poems in "The Reluctant Lady." As with the first section, these poems move from earlier to later work, but are not strictly chronological in order.

The last page of her binder contains a single typed draft of the final poem in this volume, "Next Time," in which she whimsically states a preference for her reincarnated self.

In selecting poems for this volume, I sought to represent each of the major themes of her work: portraits; theological questions; nature; relationships ("friendship, love, our interdependence in our struggle to be human," as she put it); and the interior landscape of her emotions (what she referred to somewhat wryly in her notes as "Familiar Disturbances."). I have not included work that was clearly not completed, though one could argue that, with Janet, many pieces were ever open to revision.

She was attentive to shades of connotation, and to the sounds and cadence of language and her nature was to continually question whether she had landed on the word or phrase that embodied her experienced truth. Her subtle revisions suggest that while perfection in this sense was elusive, she knew when it was being approached. And this was part of her artistic journey.

I.

Early to late (1962 – 1987)

Magic Writing

The lemon juice was easy.
"Now take it somewhere else," they said.
Behind the door
    my pen's scritch scritch
    the barely acrid air
could be nothing worth attending
Only those knowing fire
                knew me.

The Inner Child

The child who bears the scar upon my nose,
The sloping eyelid, understated hands
Weeps again, and the child-like hides
Among the fringes of my call
In some ancient, shady place
Camouflaging all except her tears
Which eat the earth and undermine
My feet in seeking her.

Where does she clutch her bounty,
Clever, crying little thief
Alone and weary of her prize?
A dampened tissue tells me she has fled.
And I must wait until my fugitive
Has greater need of me
To lure, with love, the homeless to her bed.

Envy

Heathen, how I envy you
When my soul groans and writhes
For though you feel the stabs like me
You can, with cool eye, steel yourself
To watch your virtue die.

Avowed inheritor of the kingdom,
A double thrust I must receive.
The wound itself. And knowledge that
The devil won another round
In face of light artillery.

Lady From the Prayer Group

Her eyes engrave an invitation
To a feast, "Come, join us!"
Who but the rudest could reject
The promise of such manna?

Why, then my fingers cold against
        Her fervent clasp?
Why ask myself
        Why I was asked?

Perhaps her awful wisdom views
My restless face with pity
My prayers askew
Beneath my fuzzy hat.

I'll bargain with you, Shiny Soul,
Since my emaciation stirs your heart
I'll pray I learn to pray like you
If you'll depart.

The Self-Anointed

Beware the hideously austere!
The saints alone succeeded
In glorifying wooden bed
and cold, grey food and awesome fear.
But saints are in such short supply this year.

Our self-anointed come in face
As varied as their penance.
They're sometimes seen in collars round
Or flowered figure, primly laced.
All sternly seek the promised balm of Grace.

Their zeal falls short of sacrifice
By Holy Word intended.
They take away the wonder of
Our feathered bed, our curried rice –
Then hardly ever give us Jesus Christ.

Corporate Communication

They sat, our band of Christians,
Swathed in party dress; their shoes
Like mirrors, their faces bright with Mission.
Well-groomed minds, Bible-versed
From hours of discussion agreeably admitted
The fitness of controlled dissent
And lazily, like balls across a tennis net,
Opinions came and went.

And then some reckless finger loosed a mask.
Aghast, the victim held it in his lap
And savagely – unthinking one presumes –
Cracked a chinked armor across the room.

A laggard voice sore strangled
In presence of such erudition
Began to speak, a red-faced Christian
Impatiently allowed four words (with all good grace)
Then wheeled and left her talking into space.

All evening did that velvet room abound
With the Church Militant's euphony of sound;
A plaintive solo on Purity's reward;
Then Meekness blundered in
Cherishing its voice above the din.
Humility insisted on its way
Tracing the essence of its selfless day.

Oh make a joyful noise unto the Lord!
And bring not Peace but a two-edged sword,
For the doctrine of Love may go unheard
Unless your voice has the final word.

Advent

Fifteen more shopping days
To buy
Our glittering placebos for peace.
Fifteen more days
To hide
In the maelstrom of motion and babble.

Ten more shopping days
To shroud
Ourselves in tinsel and whiskers.
Ten more days
To erase
With a "Ho-Ho-Ho" the memory of a stable.

Five more shopping days
To drink
And do our faltering dance of love.
Five more days
To dismiss
The thought of Love that conquers Hell.

One more shopping day
To listen
For one hushed, expectant moment.
One more day
To escape
The appalling promise of a miracle.

Birthday Party

Your candles that display our pagan joys
Are finally extinguished by our breath.
Your creche survives in cluttered darkness;
One king asunder on his gift of myrrh.
Hopes and fears collide and rend the air.

Have you need, dear Child, of a caress?

My arms would answer and, with order, spread
My threadbare faith upon your nakedness,
Did I not need, where I stand caroling alone,
The blessed, steadfast comfort of Your own.

Ode to Renewal

A rumor's scrawled on sidewalks.
It's blown down rancid alleys
   in swirls of litter
And into church doors, hopefully ajar
    to catch it
That Christ has taken up full residence this season
In the city.
And all who would renew things, urban-wise,
Are His disciples.
They chart their holy population trends and preach the
   gospel of a heaven
For those who scour cabbage-scented halls
   renouncing boxwoods
   and split-level heresies.
And some are called, on dust jackets,
Prophets.
Their voices rail past factories and tremble
   in the pastures;
Thread rumor through the crabgrass, along the
   golden borders of calendula
And into churches, cool and quiet
   and warm with expectation.
And the priests sigh because they have no data
   for their incense pots.
They know the path through tedium is chartless.
The God-and-Mammon ratio can't be graphed;
Nor can the incidence of facelessness
   among the beautiful.

But it is said that
    where the lawnmowers agonize
    where laughter crumbles in the air
    where hope is skewered on toothpicks
       and devoured,
Christ wipes the city from his feet
    and can be heard
       along the flagstones.

Graven Images

My pagan soul has
Idols by the score.
But each time I bow down,
As Priest of Baal
Are wont to do,
I see the outline
Of my shabby shoe.

Epitaph

Her search was sadly incomplete.
The Kingdom's keys, the widow's mite –
Befuddled, she would lose them.
Her oil lamps petered out before the night.
The rock she'd built her house upon
She'd blithely sow the seed thereon
Or stumble o'er it.
She'd scatter pearls before the swine
And then deplore it.

But trust she does,
Stone now upon her breast,
That God's eternal breath of life
Blows tares and mustard seeds alike
Unto their heavenly rest.

Dr. Adam and Ms. Eve[1]

When one Adam and Eve
(Two of millions of Adams and Eves
        who have been since the beginning)
Walked in an Eden on a Sunday afternoon
      in the fall of the year,
They believed they were viewing Creation.
Their minds had shed
      like the snake its skin
The clutter of knowledge
      that burdened their kind,
And their eyes looked with wonderment
      on the first golden forest.
They fingered the berries along the path
And pondered long upon
      their colored, coded message.
Their feet knew softness on the matted leaves
    and the hardness of the tree roots and rocks
    and the difference was remarkable to them.
When they paused by a pond
    the only geese in the world sauntered down
    the only hill in the world
And tip-toed into the water.
The ducks came, too,
And, swimming, saw Adam and Eve on the bank
    and came to display their orange feet
    and the artistry of their recently designed
    phenomenal feathers.
They heralded their arrival with a sound
    that made the humans laugh into the sky
Where soaring buzzards balanced it on their wings.
But they did not laugh for the first time that day

For they had carried laughter with them
in their hands
and in their pockets
and in their eyes.
But when they left the Garden, Adam said,
"Eden was not a good place."
Eve was startled, and she asked,
"Why, Adam?
We disobeyed no one
Ate of nothing forbidden.
We were not driven out.
The guards were benevolent."
"You don't understand," replied Adam,
"being constructed merely of a rib."
"I understand that we were happy," she said.
To which he replied,
"Happiness is an illusion and a snare."
"Where is that written?" frowned Eve
begging the issue with ancient accuracy.
Adam's face darkened, and Eve covered herself
with fig leaves
Having discovered suddenly
that she was naked.

Riddle

No new phenomenon
Yet always revelation.
It shuns the heart
And leaves great indentation.
No cure is known.

Evades square root
Abhors examination
Suffers monumentally
Is subject to temptation.
Yet much extolled.

Its strength defies all words
Its worth, evaluation.
It seeks much room
Yet fiercely shuns privation.

Noble, Grasping
Encompassing, Exclusive
Truthful, Mystifying
Dependable, Elusive.

Yet it is claimed
Its power of seduction
Will save the world
From mass destruction.

Spinster

Dispel your anguish, maid. Rejoice!
The mirror's tales of doom are lies.
The graying, parchment portraiture
You view with enmity is friend
And savior in disguise. The veined hands
Open door to your release
For, with your waning Spring, desire dies.

"Shovels"[2]

He comes to church now that
Sundays, Mondays, Tuesdays
Are not a potpourri of whiskey-laden
Hours of wandering sleep.
Sun-sodden, shade-drenched
He has rediscovered coat and matching trousers
Too light in weight for winter pilgrimages
Not dark enough for fashion's nod
This time of year.

But his shoes are brilliant
As a financiers'
And his eyes are gentle
For reasons of his own
And he wears a red carnation
In his buttonhole.
This, in weekly ritual, he gives to me.
For all the gems of liturgy, I would not trade
This moment when he becomes "m' Lord"
And I his Lady.

Silence

There is the golden kind
That wisdom spawns
And love, by mutual consent,
Subscribes to.
The other, mercilessly dumb,
Makes decibels the heart records
And a self that one must
Die to.

Thoughts on Current Non-Conformity

His beard awash in coffee cup
He flays the world's monotony;
Gray flannel suit, religious creed.
And wonders why he goes awry;
His feathered jabs paid little heed.

Ask poet, artist, Thespian
On revolutionary binge
Why *he* is free from
Established bounds to part.
The answer is:
He only tries to bastardize
When he has learned the form of art.

The Cloak

If you must hate
Don't be vile about it.
Don't swear
And grimace
And shout.
There is a way.
You must smile about it.

You'll need a veranda
And a rocking chair
And a clean white hankie
And tidy hair.

Thus dignified, you're free to loathe
All threats that 'yond the pillars loom.
And swear, with genteel fervor, that
The only odor in the world
Is that of climbing-vines in bloom.

Friend

Lovingly you pressed my face
Into the sodden pillow
Of your own despair.
Trusting that the love
You glimpsed in me
Would breathe new life
On barren places there.
But in my imperfection
I came up for air.

Pigeons

You tryst in the shadows
Puffed up and beady eyed
Murmuring in the girders
Trains slamming above, you
Gracelessly flap and float
From trestle to ground.
Your cousins in white belfries
Aloft on sacred sounds
Would denounce you.
Circling every shoe in sight!
Strutting on the fouled bricks
In your dirty clothes
And your gawdy pink feet.

My Neighbor's Garden

We share a boundary, she and I,
With opening enough in foliage
For me to see the beauty she creates.
Statuesque, she moves about her garden
Wand in hand. With magical agility
She woos her flowers into blooming
While I, on my side, pull and whack and drench
My own into a shape
Of mere respectability.
She snips and snips –
Then bears her choice inside
Where miracles emerge from jars and vases.
My neighbor loves her flowers so profoundly
That she fences them about with screams
That slash the languid air
And set my own heart pounding.
Her little girl stands rigid with confusion
Against the sweet profusion
Of her mother's garden.

The Snapshot

She thrust it in a drawer, this half-glimpsed picture
of her son at twilight, kneeling by his boy
(minute in blue and posing smartly).
Nothing in view but the snow piled high
in the fading light around them, down the long street and past
    the brooding houses.
The man crouching there in his great black coat
could have been a father/uncle/cousin
from her own frozen north,
all of them in far gone albums.
Only this hatless man now, his fine familiar head
in artless silhouette against the snow
    and dying sun.
Why then did she, a veteran of the cold,
leave it thawing in a drawer?
Would she have felt less had the day been young
and everything greening?

Antiphonal Reading
(New Year's Eve)[3]

To remember the hunger and hopelessness of people whose lives
rarely touch ours, and to help when it is within our power. But
not to become so absorbed in the woes of mankind that we are
unable to see the person next to us who is in need.

> To perceive the wonder of the world. To enjoy each
> moment because that is all we are guaranteed.

To be unafraid to show gentleness for it seems to be a fact of
life that it is where our greatest strengths are found.

> To try to learn the secret of giving and taking. Each
> person needs to strike his own balance. If we do either
> one too much, we don't feel happy and neither does
> anyone else.

To love pure knowledge but not to lust after it lest it become
a tyrant, shutting out the learning that seeks to bewitch us
through our senses. To remember that some things do not give
up their mystery to microscopes and test tubes.

> To have dreams. They are what keep hope alive. To
> know, too, when to give one up that we have worn out or
> outgrown – and then to spin another.

To learn to trust our own perceptions and to have the courage
to act on them.

To leave spaces in our lives for thinking quietly about things and how they all fit together.

To keep a firm hand on the love of power and money and flattery as sources of nourishment, knowing they are capricious seducers that vanish without warning.

To be glad that we're all different – different skins, different dispositions, different ways of viewing the world. Maybe then we won't be so afraid of each other. For fear is fertile ground for hatred – and the world is saturated with that, and does not need the stubborn ounces of our own.

To laugh more this year. There are probably more reasons to do it than we usually notice.

We have not, without cause, been labeled "the Human Comedy." Our little dreams of good intentions and vain pretensions should at least make us smile.

Epitaph [4]

She grasped the flight of geese
    far better than the galaxies
dutifully admired* spring but
    secretly belonged to fall.

---

*   *"gave obeisance (?) to spring"* written in margin of hardcopy (ed.)

2.

Haiku and Senryu

Lone boy on skateboard
Twists and leaps in mid-day.
What, no school?

Seven shouting crows,
Weathervanes on winter trees
Momentarily...

In the unspoiled sky
One raggedy, playful cloud
Defaces the moon.

Whooping and trilling,
Crayon-colored whirl-i-gigs,
Girls on snow walk.

That old curmudgeon oak
Rattles last year's leaves
At giddy daffodils.

After the night wind,
Platoons of daffodils
Aghast upon the ground.

Mussy with sleep,
My draped cat dreams
Of endless languor.

Nuns in prudent shoes,
Crosses swinging, tolling time
Inexorably...

Leaves, tip to trunk,
Clutching the branch, shouting gold,
Ginkgoes taunt the wind.

Geese possess the sky
Ambiguously crying:
Come home! Farewell!

3.

The Reluctant Lady
and other poems

Eulogy for Leaves

Your gold must surely be
Medals for your dying.
I, too, would rouge my cheeks
Against the killer's breath
Had I your flair for travesty,
And cakewalk to *my* death!

Insomnia

Four o'clock. An acorn drops
An impish note into the pause
Where tree toads yawn.
The moon rests weary elbows on the sill
And sighs for dawn.
And I, on endless vigil, seek to find
A phantom document
Among the archives of my mind.

The Bishop's Lady

Her face seems always bathed in candlelight
As though she hears a private tune inside
And is in love with destiny.
And those who come within the beam
Discern the meaning of her gentle might
For she wears her goodness lightly
Leaving others free to be.

Despair

He etches paths across my face
To make me permanently his –
This creature who takes room and board
Within me.
He nibbles at the edges of my hope.
And though nightly I eradicate
His handiwork with creams,
Still, he maintains his stubborn vigil
Curled up amidst the drama of my dreams.

Occasionally this egotist decides
That his talents justify a fuller range
And, amenities neglected, he departs.
But the climate of my house
Suits his tastes so perfectly
That he returns to lay his head upon my heart.

Antique Show

She murmurs knowingly
Among the porcelain.
Painted and glazed, they fuse,
Man-made and Man,
And must possess each other.
Her gloved hand on a drawer knob
In search of sulking prices
Will hold, at the propitious time,
The pen that pledges
Countless heavens.
Perhaps this time
They will be more than
Plate and desk
Among the cinders.

The Nuns

I like to watch the nuns go by,
A bevy of solemnity.
Heads immured in starchy casts
Turn to talk
With lyric ease.
Indiscreetly, breezes press
Sacred robes
On flexing knees.
Swish, swish they pass
In prudent shoes,
Crosses swinging with each step,
Tolling time
Inexorably.

Query

Does He watch our tribal dance
To Self – our vulgar praise –
With gentle mirth;
He who stitched outlandish† lace
Along the boist'rous surf?

---

†   Other descriptors for lace considered: *such dainty; a dainty; fastidious; such fussy; buffoonish; exquisite; effete*

Winter Sabbath, 4 O'Clock

Well, here we are again, God, in your haunted church,
Ghosts of the program rustlers and pew kickers
Stripped sanctuary, Naked soul. How awkwardly I make
  amends.
Must we go through life like quarrelsome lovers, You and I;
Hungering, knocking, answering too early and too late?
But my heart is as persistent as Your patience.
I will call again today down that dark tunnel in this dimming
  church,
Daring to hope that I shall finally hear the saving difference
Between my own voice echoing in my ears
And Your voice thundering like the surf against my foolish will.

The Reluctant Lady[5]

Spring shivers long this year
In anxious buds

Uses green experimentally
Dabs and spatters,
Bullies the mercury.

Frugally dispatches birds
Alerted for retreat
Lest her annual idea
This time prove obsolete.

To My Child

I would wrap you in yards of summer hours,
Coerce the sun and exorcise the rain.
I have trinkets in my magic purse
To hypnotize you so that, waking,
You will believe what isn't so again.
And I have words, oh words enough
To cover every homily with shame.
But I must learn to close the door, my child
And leave you with the gift I would withhold:
The privilege of pain.

The Wake

To a Friend Who Sorrows

To place the silverware in ranks
Of mourning on the cloth
Beside the ham, beside the salad
Tossed with loving, frenzied haste;
To bleach the pit-black coffee with the cream
And sprinkle color on this mound and that
And plant a parsley spray,

My hands are eager, fingertips aloft
Like those that knit and knit
The endless rows of scarfing that
Can only warm a loved one in
A temporary chrysalis.

I wished to say to you above
The sawdust food held on your knee,
"Just let me take with me today
That angular piece of pain I see
Tucked in the dark behind your eyes.
I have no loneliness in store this week
And I'd be more than glad..."

Instead, of course, I put the scraps
Of mangled food into the bag
Where feeble benedictions go
And left you for another day.

The Derelict[6]

The old man's tears seeped through
The shale of his confusion
And bogus reasons snarled in his tongue.
Someone whispered that it was his way
To weep beside his fantasies; to wander there among
The cauldrons of his mind
And heal his shapeless wounds with magic remedies.
You'd see that he'd be laughing soon.

Well, laugh, old man. Expose
Your tears as counterfeit
And join the crowd of Janus faces.
Somewhere behind the sting we know
That water never flows from arid places.

The Wind[7]

The wind is far too eloquent for sleep tonight.
On daylight spree, it reeled and prattled in the tops of trees
And swooped to puppy chasing. The mind could overlook
Its fey inanities.

Tonight, with calloused palms, it grapples with my stubborn
    house
And shouts its virile victories to the loins.
From places where the senses lurk it comes and speaks
Of rendezvous where only the surrendered self is flung.

Seduction

Like wanton women we scan the room
For a beholder, and dangle
Baubles of ourselves before
A myriad sightless eyes.

Consummating futilely
Until the Master Lover wraps
Our tinsel round His hand
And saves us from our promiscuity.

The Buber Conundrum[8]

If you became the "I" of which
The "I" of me was "It,"
And if your "I" became a "Thou"
To which my "It" meant quite a bit.
Then you encountered "Thou" in me
And I was "I" because of thee,
Then "I" would be by "Thou" confused
And ask what brand of tea you used.

Narcissa

Who will mend the pieces, Lord,
When the dance is done?
When the pirouetting falters
And applause, once won,
Now fades and viewers file
Through the lighted doors?
Who will bend to sweep
The dresden-splintered floor
And weep to see the ballerina
On her knees?
Who will mend the pieces, Lord?
Thee?

Hell

The trees are chafed by timeless winds
That sear the face of snowmen
Broomstick arms outspread
Eternally denied embrace.
This is where the winter sun
Twinkles and deceives and blinds.
Through everlasting Januarys
Music clutches horn and string
And words are frozen in the mind.
Footprints wander maze on maze
Into a nonexistent spring.

A fire's crackle would intrude.
No flames enfold the silence
That is granted here.
For hell is cold.

Rehabilitation

Considering the fix we're in
What with the Fall
And Original Sin
And killing God
Not too long after
All that fratricide,
It's quite exhilarating
(Heroic, you might say)
This chummy rehabilitating
Basket-weaving therapy
We homicides
Take part in every day.

("You sew my key case.
I'll shape your clay.")

Man, 1978 [9]

His fear screams godward
But the air is dead
Like the silence after love's retreat.
His gods have fled.

A Resolution[10]

In our encounter
Let me bear in mind
That all who like to sip
Don't soak in wine:
And should a crass integrity
Prod me to expose the depths of me,
Let me recall, in my elation,
That mercy stands above
Self-revelation.
And I will try to show my love
In manner more benign,
And leave you with your fantasies –
And me with mine.

A Thought[II]

A fragment of a shattered heart can be
A knife to lance another's idiocy.

A Letter

Frostbitten words
Their meaning blurred
By blizzard winds
Of your capricious temperament.
They hold my body in their glacial grip
Until the warm hands of remembrance
Thaw them into tears.

Has science yet discovered
How far below the freezing point
Love can survive?
Has precept been defied?

How strange the cold should
Merely fix the shape.

Scars

The flesh forgets its wounds.
The startled blood retreats,
Closing a pale, numb door behind.
Our lips, alone, recall –
And they, with some delight –
Our caricature of pain.

The heart has memory of its own.
One blow and it is doomed
To endless shocks that reason shuns;
Its frail scar opened by
A hand's remark, the slant of light,
A certain kind of rain.

To J.E. 12

I

I will my self to ice
To keep the lovely flakes
You snow upon me.
But blood plots a different device;
Becomes your friend, me enemy.

II

And when I tell you
I have come to love
Your dauntlessness
    your dear buffoonery
That wraps you tight against my view
You will, unflinchingly,
Allow me to transform you
    into father.
Your task renewed
    to probe its sorcery.

Be gentle, friend,
For I am older now and watched
Eternities of pale affections
    come and go
And still am not immune to slaughter.
So wear your softest wings
    I ask
The hour you nudge me
Down the darkening path
    as daughter.

The Blue Water Tower
(Interstate 95)

No doubt some recently bicepted boy-turned-seraphim
    rose in exultation and fluttered there to write
    in letters taller than a man is, "Sharon I love you. Me."
    in celestial white.

Tomorrow someone else, brim-full of me
    and old bones hallowed for the climb
    will sway (necktie snatching at the wind)
    up the blue legs and ...
    like a god gone awry...
    splash with white the startled sky

And ever after
    those careening past will all wear a smile
    and wonder who I am for about a mile.

Next Time

Next time I will be a pond
Where life spawns murkily
In blips and gurgles
And on whose face lily pads lounge

Where people bend to see their faces
Framed in borrowed clouds
And bending grasses
And see them selves
The way they had in mind.[‡]

<hr />

[‡] The poem rendered here is based on a typed final draft. However, an earlier
handwritten version provides this substitute for the final two lines:
So precisely the perfection
They had in mind.

No doubt — — — — — — — — — — boy-friend or — — —
— — — — — — — —
to — — — — — — — — — — — —

Next time, — — — I will be a friend
Whose life — — — — — — — — — — — nearby
for blips & gurgles.
— — — —
And — — — — — — — — — —
When — people — — to see their faces
framed in clouds and — — — — — —
And — — — — the way   So — — — — — — —
— — — — — — —   Thy — — — — — —

— — — in — — — — — — life — — — — — —
for — — — & gurgles
And — — — — face
— — — — — — — .
And — — — — — — — my — — —
— — — — — — into my face
(— — — — — — — clouds)
And
— — — — — — — — —
— — — — — — .

When — — — — — — — — — —
an blips and gurgles

End Notes

Janet annotated some poems to frame the pieces as part of a poetry reading, probably in the late 1970s. Her notes appear in quotations.

---

1   *Dr. Adam and Ms. Eve.* "This [one] is a parable. The Sunday walk referred to was an event in the life of a relationship – the rest speaks to the perils of communication, and maybe even a couple of other things. It's status as a poem may depend a bit heavily on the skill of the typesetter. But *that's* not without precedent..."

2   *"Shovels."* Never formally titled as such, this is a portrait of the eponymous man who frequently visited St Andrew's Church, and whom Janet, unsurprisingly, befriended. (ed.)

3   *Antiphonal Reading.* In the form of New Year resolutions, this was originally spoken (alternately by a voice from the front and a voice from the back) by Janet Hickman and Luke Mette, December 1975 at the Unitarian Church, Wilmington, Delaware. A member of congregation, Betty Carota, obtained a copy of text, which was sent to Pat O'Toole, with a kind note, after Janet's death in 2006. (ed.)

4   *Epitaph.* Unlike the poem, above, by this same title (possibly a portrait of a departed church-goer Janet knew), this epitaph is, I think, self-referential. Written on the reverse side of a penned draft of *"Next Time,"* which concludes this collection. (ed.)

5   *The Reluctant Lady.* "Sometimes spring teases us, makes us believe she's really on the way, and then stops dead in her tracks leaving us chilled in the midst of her unfinished business."

6   *The Derelict.* "...[W]ritten after a bewildering attempt on my part to discover why an old man had suddenly started crying at a public event. I was told by someone next to me to forget it – that his tears meant nothing.

7   *The Wind.* In a poetry reading event, Janet read this poem followed by "Insomnia" and maybe one other. Here is how she introduced this segment of her reading (ed.) "I have a category here called Familiar Disturbances. I suppose I could have included romantic love in this, but I'll do those later and just stick with depression and insomnia this time around."

8   *A Buber Conundrum.* "This...is a bit of whimsy written after discovering Martin Buber, the noted theologian. He makes the distinction between really knowing the other in an "I-Thou" relationship as opposed to knowing about the other in an "I-It" encounter in which the other is viewed as a phenomenon. This is a ridiculous simplification of a lengthy and profound theological treatise. So is the poem."

9   *Man, 1978* "Four lines on the ways things seen to be for our skeptical, contemporary human race."

10   *A Resolution* "...was written before 'letting it all hang out' became a talisman of the human potential movement. I seem to have remained unscathed – which may have something to say about old dogs and new tricks. At any rate here is my pact with you."

11   *An Observation.* "Here is a quick observation on one of the ways we co-exist."

12   *To J. E.* "It's acceptable to idealize your therapist – it's another face of love though doomed to the annals of the unrequited. I found the experience important enough to write about, and here are two poems."

About the Editor

Stewart Hickman is a writer based in Maryland (USA). He has most recently published a chapbook of his own poetry, *why i never got to neptune* (Ptarmigan House, Sept 2022). *Out and Back*, his first chapbook of poems and short essays, is dedicated to his mother. www.StewartHickman.com

www.ingramcontent.com/pod-product-compliance
Lightning Source LLC
Chambersburg PA
CBHW070442130626
46553CB00006B/2275

* 9 7 9 8 9 8 5 7 3 9 3 2 9 *